Dalai Lama - visiting the
Internat... l
... 2018
Rishike...

J x.

CW00493935

HAPPINESS

HAPPINESS

His Holiness
the Dalai Lama

PENGUIN BOOKS
An imprint of Penguin Random House

PENGUIN BOOKS

USA | Canada | UK | Ireland | Australia
New Zealand | India | South Africa | China

Penguin Books is part of the Penguin Random House group of companies whose addresses can be found at global.penguinrandomhouse.com

Published by Penguin Random House India Pvt. Ltd
7th Floor, Infinity Tower C, DLF Cyber City,
Gurgaon 122 002, Haryana, India

Penguin Random House India

First published in Penguin Books by Penguin Random House India 2018

Copyright © The Dalai Lama Foundation 2018

All rights reserved

10 9 8 7 6 5 4 3 2 1

The views and opinions expressed in this book are the author's own and the facts are as reported by him which have been verified to the extent possible, and the publishers are not in any way liable for the same.

ISBN 9780670090921

For sale in India only

Typeset in Adobe Garamond Pro by Manipal Digital Systems, Manipal
Printed at Replika Press Pvt. Ltd, India

This book is sold subject to the condition that it shall not, by way of trade or otherwise, be lent, resold, hired out, or otherwise circulated without the publisher's prior consent in any form of binding or cover other than that in which it is published and without a similar condition including this condition being imposed on the subsequent purchaser.

www.penguin.co.in

FSC www.fsc.org
MIX
Paper from responsible sources
FSC® C016779

Dear brothers and sisters, I am very happy to have this opportunity to talk to you.

~

Whenever I give a talk, I always have this feeling that we human beings are all the same—mentally, emotionally and physically. Everyone wants a happy life.

Nobody wakes up in the morning wishing for more trouble that day. However, emotional trouble is essentially our own creation. I think it is largely due to two things. The first is lack of knowledge of reality due to absence of a holistic view and the second is a self-centred attitude.

~

These two things—lack of knowledge and a self-centred attitude—create unnecessary problems. We can't blame our problems on anybody or anything else. Ultimately we have to realize that the cause of these problems lies within ourselves. So how do we deal with them?

~

We deal with them not through prayer, not through money, not through power, but through understanding and awareness—what we may call wisdom.

~

Happiness. Everyone, including animals, wants less mental disturbance. So do we human beings of course. But before talking about the source of happiness, it might be useful to know something about the system of our minds. Just like pleasure, pain is also part of our experiences. Usually people are under the impression that the mind is independent, absolute. Science, too, is not yet clear about the distinction between the sensorial mind and consciousness.

~

It is important to make that distinction. When people seek pleasurable experiences, they rely mainly on the sensorial level to attain that pleasure—watching something beautiful, listening to music, tasting or smelling something. This includes tactile pleasures, including sex. These five are positive experiences mainly at the sensorial level; they are temporary. The object of beauty you behold or the beautiful music you hear is gone the moment you stop seeing or hearing it.

~

Nevertheless, if you develop a mental level with certain positive experiences, the experience of pleasure lasts longer. So a disturbing noise at the sensorial level will not affect this basic calmness. Even the pain of physical illness can be subdued in this state. On the other hand, no sensorial pleasure can be had if the basic mental state is that of fear, anxiety and stress. Obviously, mental-level experiences are more important than sensorial ones.

~

It is important to understand that mental-level happiness need not be about pleasure. It's about mental satisfaction or fulfilment. Even physical suffering and pain can bring deep satisfaction at the mental level. Happiness mainly refers to this feeling at the level of consciousness.

~

All major religious traditions try to bring about calmness, peacefulness and positivity at the mental level. Faith is not at the sensorial level. It is the sixth consciousness. Of course, the sensorial level helps in attaining mental satisfaction, for example, seeing the image of the Buddha or a god, or listening to prayers. However, the real effect is due to faith. The practice of love, compassion, and with them, forgiveness, tolerance and contentment, operate at the systemic level of consciousness.

~

There are non-theistic religious traditions, such as a part of Sankhya, a 3000-year-old Indian tradition, and Jainism and Buddhism that do not talk about a creator, but believe instead in the law of causality or the law of cause and effect.

~

Everybody in this country knows about the law of karma. It means action. Any action—whether physical, verbal or mental—arising out of any positive emotion or sincere motivation, like compassion and forgiveness, is positive or good karma. Since the motivation is good, there's a sense of concern for others' well-being, which, as it benefits others and oneself, is considered positive. Otherwise, there's no absolute positive or negative. For example, anger, hatred and suspicion are considered negative. Suspicion maybe positive or negative. Negative is that which is uncomfortable to oneself and/or to others. Any such motivation will lead to physical, verbal or mental action that can produce negative karma. Experiences of pleasure, pain and the action that causes them constitute the law of causality.

Both Jainism and Buddhism may have different approaches to many aspects of life but the fundamental purpose is the same: to enhance our ability to love and forgive, and to be compassionate in day-to-day life.

~

Theistic religions use the concept of god or the creator. On the other hand, non-theistic traditions use the concept of the law of causality. They believe that if you are good to others, you will benefit, and if you harm others, you will suffer negative consequences. Interestingly, there is also another way. Without touching upon the mysterious aspects of religions, by only looking at the obvious ones, we can educate people about compassion and how it can lead to happiness.

~

First, biologically, all social animals show a sense of responsibility towards their group. The reality is that individual survival and well-being depend upon the welfare of the group. Because of this reality, every individual has a sense of community. No matter how powerful, no individual can survive alone, let alone be happy. His very survival depends on the rest of his community. That's a fact. Because of that, there must be some emotion that produces affection and brings community members close to each other.

~

While compassion brings a community closer, anger does the opposite. Anger and fear, which push an individual away from his community, are harmful for survival. Of course, fear can be positive too—as a defence against danger as it produces caution. So at the emotional level we are wired to protect ourselves and our interests, and to expel the opposite. Affection and compassion are part of our psyche, intended to help us survive. It is the same with dogs, cats and birds. Humans though have this marvellous intelligence. On the basis of our biological and emotional potential, we should use our intelligence for long-term interests. With a wider perspective of interest, we can then increase our compassion, towards which we are naturally inclined.

~

The biological wiring for love and compassion is limited, biased and often accompanied by hatred and suspicion. Nevertheless, if we are trained to use it with intelligence, reason and logic for a longer term and with a broader perspective, it could certainly become unbiased. We develop a biological compassion towards a friend and hatred towards an enemy, because it is oriented towards another's attitude. If your friend has a good attitude towards you, you love him. On the other hand, your antagonist's attitude is harmful. Therefore, you hate him. Now use your intelligence. Irrespective of whether someone is your friend or an enemy, that person is still a part of your community. Your life depends on the community. Not everyone is necessarily your friend. However, you need each other for survival. An old way of thinking was 'we' and 'they', with a solid barrier in between. 'We' don't care about 'them'. In ancient times, each nation was more or less independent. Today, everything is interdependent. So that feeling of 'we' and 'they' is outdated.

~

We must consider the rest of the world and humanity as part of 'we', because our interest depends on everyone else's. There's no relevance here of personal attitude. Using this reasoning, we can extend our genuine sense of concern and well-being to others because they are a part of our community. We can orient ourselves towards them as brothers and sisters of our community; we can extend our love and compassion to them. An animal can't do that. We human beings can use our intelligence to do that. We have the potential to develop that level of compassion. That is unbiased, genuine compassion. It is important to make a distinction here.

~

If your so-called adversary creates a problem for you, you may take an appropriate countermeasure as far as action is concerned. But as a human being, you can still continue to be compassionate and have a sense of concern for his well-being. In fact, out of genuine concern for his well-being, if you let his wrongdoings go unchecked, ultimately he will suffer. So take that countermeasure in order to stop him from doing anything wrong. While it's a countermeasure, it is also an act of compassion. So this is a way of training our mind not through meditation but by utilizing our intelligence. Once we develop this mental attitude, based on reason and open-mindedness, we can be happy. Here happiness means a peaceful mind, which is devoid of stress, anxiety or fear. On one level, you can see negative things, but at a deeper level, you can still be calm, irrespective of whether you are a believer or a non-believer. Science speaks of a close link between a healthy body and a healthy mind.

An agitated mind over a long period of time can be very harmful to one's physical well-being. A calm, healthy mind is extremely beneficial for physical health. Fear, anger and hatred actually eat into our immune system. On the other hand, a less stressful mind is extremely helpful in maintaining good physical health.

~

I would like to share with you an incident that happened in

New York City during a meeting of medical scientists and other people. One of the scientists mentioned that according to his findings, people who express themselves frequently using 'I', 'me', 'mine' have a greater risk of having heart attacks. These people are too self-centred; such an attitude makes even a small problem unbearable. Once you open your heart to others' well-being, which I call the opening of your inner door, you can communicate with other people easily. This will help you make more friends, reduce feelings of loneliness and develop feelings of compassion, which reduces anxiety. And that is useful for our health. After all, we are social animals and such an attitude goes well with our reality.

~

Generally, people stress on the importance of education. They are right. Many problems arise due to lack of knowledge and ignorance. Education can equip you to develop a broader, comprehensive and more holistic perspective. Education should reduce the gap between appearance and reality. Everybody understands the importance of education. On the basis of scientific findings, we know that positive emotions are important for our health, for a happy individual, a happy family, and a happy community. This I consider the real art of happiness.

I've learnt this through personal experience.

~

I'm seventy-six years old now.[1] I lost my freedom at as early an age as sixteen. At the age of twenty-four, I became a refugee. A stateless, homeless individual. While I lost a small home in Tibet, I found a big home in India.

[1] The Dalai Lama delivered this lecture in 2011.

Throughout my life, I have gone through turbulence but my mind continues to remain peaceful not through dullness, I hope [laughs]. Moreover, I feel that my mind is quite sharp. When I engage with famous scientists, my knowledge is almost zero compared to theirs, but we logically analyse every single point. That helps sharpen the mind. So I hope my mind is not that dull. However, during these turbulent times, my mind is calm. The immediate result is that my health is good except that an important organ, the gall bladder, is gone. So while this human body looks normal, there's one important organ missing. Basically my health is very good. My mental state, I think, is what makes the difference. My physician friends tell me my physical condition is not like that of a seventy-plus man, and that I seem ten years younger. Some introduce me as a reincarnation of the Bodhisattva, but I know

I am no higher being or anyone like that. I know my own mind. I can read my own mind. I am a human being who utilizes his intelligence properly. The result is a mentally happy, physically healthy human being. Everybody has the same potential. The only thing is whether they pay attention or not, whether they have sufficient awareness or not; that is the point. Otherwise, all of us have the same potential.

~

I think ancient Indian treasures have detailed knowledge of human emotions, of the human mind. So, naturally, regardless of whether it is Jainism, Buddhism or Hinduism, all religions have a common practice of *samadhan* and vipassana, both of which involve mental training. Since these traditions follow these practices, they follow a map of the mind. I think that needs to be taught more. It should be part of an academic subject. Western psychology is very limited. The world of the mind is so vast; it is very important to know the system, to know different minds and how they develop and work. For medical knowledge, you need to know the body and how it works. For mental awareness too we need to study the system of the mind as an academic subject and not as a religious subject. If that knowledge is used to attain heaven (or hell!) in the afterlife, it becomes a religious thing. If it's used to attain well-being in this life, it has nothing to do with religion. I often tease my Indian friends. When one worships one's god or goddess every day with incense sticks and flowers, and recites Sanskrit shlokas without knowing their meanings, it's of no use.

~

We must pay more attention and study this rich ancient Indian thought. India is a religious nation. I often say that religious faith and unjust actions cannot go together. There is no third choice. There are only two—religious-minded carrying on an honest, just, truthful life, or leading a corrupt life, denying god, denying karma, and just seeking money and power. This, the 'third choice'—being both religious and corrupt, is a big contradiction. Pray to Shiva, Ganesha, and in the meantime, have no hesitation in being corrupt.

~

Whether it is made up of believers or non-believers, society should be clean, transparent; when everybody is happy, a nation can be built more rapidly. Where there is a lot of corruption and injustice, poor people suffer the most. From the viewpoint of national interest, India is the second most populated nation, and has shown great stability in the last sixty years because of its vibrant democracy and rule of law. The citizens of this country should think about how to build a healthy nation. Each individual has a moral responsibility to build India in a more healthy way. Only then can this country truly make a significant impact on the world, commensurate with its size and history.

Q&A

Q: What is the difference between self-love and self-centredness?

A: A strong sense of self is necessary to develop determination and willpower. My favourite prayer is—'So long as space remains, so long as suffering remains, I will remain in order to serve them.'

~

In order to develop courage, you need to have a strong sense of self. It's very necessary. In order to combat a self-centred negative attitude, you need self-confidence. The sense of self combined with ignorance and short-sightedness is wrong.

~

Q: You talk a lot about compassion and happiness. If I am compassionate but someone I love dearly is in pain, how can I be happy?

A: A great, ancient Indian master of Buddhism once raised this question. Nobody wants pain but if you practise compassion effectively, you will feel disturbed only for a short period of time when you find someone ill or going through a painful experience. In such situations, your mental pain overwhelms you and you feel helpless because it hasn't come about voluntarily.

~

An excessive sense of concern for others' well-being causes discomfort. This happens voluntarily. You should try to develop that sense of responsibility.

~

So in it your self-confidence will give you the courage to care for another person's well-being. A weak self cannot care for another being. Concern for others can spread to the whole of humanity. To all living beings.

~

India has a very good culture of vegetarianism. In the early sixties, when I was passing through Dharamsala on the way to the Jammu airport, chicken could not be bought anywhere. Nowadays, every small restaurant serves chicken dishes in the name of progress. In Bengaluru too, I noticed chicken being served with vegetables. People consider chicken to be like vegetables. There is no feeling for their pain. In the summers, when it's very hot, the chicken sit shrivelled up in their cages, likewise in winters. It's very sad. Of course, I am a non-vegetarian. I have reasons. I gave it up in 1965 and was a strict vegetarian for a couple of months. During that period, following the advice of my Indian friend, I ate a lot of nuts. The result was that in 1966, I developed a gall bladder problem. Then I think for at least three–four weeks, I fell seriously ill and my whole body turned yellow. At that time, I truly became a living Buddha—completely yellow. Not through spiritual practice but through illness. My doctors advised me to go back to my original diet. So that's my story. We made all Tibetan monasteries' common kitchens completely vegetarian about ten–fifteen years ago. When I was fourteen and in Tibet, I made all Tibetan government festivals vegetarian; they were traditionally non-vegetarian. Also, across our settlements in India, we do not have any kind of poultry, piggery, or fishery business. We are trying to promote vegetarianism. We need a worldwide movement.

~

About compassion—on the surface, you will be disturbed, but deep inside, you will get more self-confidence, inner strength and voluntarily take on others' pain, and later you will get deeper satisfaction.

~

Q: In our pursuit of happiness, we've heard about bad things like cruelty to animals, and in our lowest moments, such thoughts have haunted us. How do we stop or delete such negative thoughts from our minds?

A: If you are angry, you will get mad; when you cannot find their weak spots, then you might hit them, but in the process your own hand might get hurt. Instead, be patient and compassionate. On 10 March 2008, I had the same experience as that on 10 March 1959—helplessness, anxiety and fear. But during the 2008 experience, I deliberately developed the practice of give and take. Visualize the Chinese officials, take their anger, fear and give my spirit of forgiveness and compassion to them. It brought me immense happiness. It did not solve the problem but my mind was calm. Anger destroys your peace of mind and eventually affects your health. Be compassionate and your mind will stay clear. Think along these lines and you can develop full conviction. I should not let anger or hatred disturb me. I must promote and cherish my positive emotions. Then comes the effort, which can take days, weeks, months, years or decades. Then your mental state will change. That much I can tell you through my own little experience.

~

Q: Twenty years ago, I had asked you in Majorca what we should do as doctors when a patient is going to die. But now I want to ask you what should a patient do to be happy when he is ill?

A: It depends on your attitude. If you believe in god, you will believe that you are a creature of god. God is all-knowing and infinitely loving, so your illness might have a meaning. If you believe in the law of causality, you will feel that today's problems are the result of your past, negative karma. Since karma is your own creation, if you create another, stronger, more positive karma, then the effect of the negative karma will reduce. So in some way, you will still have control. For a non-believer, there's another way. Shantideva[2] had suggested that when you face a problem or have painful experiences, the situation should be analysed. If it can be overcome, there's no need to worry, an effort needs to be made. If there's no way to overcome it, there's no need to worry either. Too much worry is self-torture. Better to forget. It's not

[2] Shantideva was a Buddhist scholar at Nalanda University in the eighth century AD.

easy but is a realistic approach to face a problem. More than ten years ago, I developed a painful intestinal problem. That day I was in Bihar. I was passing through a village. I saw many poor children without shoes. In Patna, I saw an ailing old man on a bed, abandoned. In my hotel, I was in pain all night long but in my mind, I could only see the children and the old man. My mind was diverted to their misery out of a sense of *karuna* or compassion, and my own physical pain felt less severe. Think more about others' well-being then your own problem and sickness will feel less painful. Otherwise, I don't know.

~

Q: I was wondering whether the request for not raising a political question comes from His Holiness or the organizers. Politics does have an impact on our happiness in these times. Does justice form a constituent of the compassion you talk about?

A: Justice is at the level of action. Compassion is the motivation. It essentially means how to take care of others' well-being. So with that mental attitude there's no place to lie, no place to exploit or harm someone. You are taking care of their well-being. Lying for the greater good. For example, Buddhist monastic practices mention that when a monk witnesses animals disappearing into the jungle and lies to a hunter later that he does not know about them, it is okay. A half-lie would be to say that he saw a bird go that way. That would be okay too. A lie is a physical, verbal action. Whether it's positive or negative depends upon our motivation. I was once asked whether corruption was okay if it was to procure jobs for a large group of people. Sincere, compassionate motivation; so here I would say positive corruption [laughs]. So purpose and motivation are important. I have already retired from political responsibility. I voluntarily, happily, proudly handed it over to the elected political leadership, so if today anyone asks me a political question I happily say that I've retired. So I have more freedom. If I want to answer, I do, otherwise I say I've retired [laughs].

~

Q: What is your definition of god and how does one experience god?

A: I was once asked by a westerner whether I'd seen Jesus Christ and I said yes. I want to know what god is. It is a mystery. Some things are beyond our thoughts; they are inconceivable. The Buddha was an enlightened human being of the highest level, someone beyond our thoughts. Originally, he was just like us; step by step, he improved his mental state. That process we can study and understand logically. Anyway, I think modern science can neither prove nor disprove god. It remains a mystery.